THE FARAWAY NORTH

Previously published in this series:

Lord Peter and Little Kerstin

Warrior Lore

THE FARAWAY NORTH

Scandinavian Ballads

translated and introduced by

IAN CUMPSTEY

Northern Displayers, Skadi Press

CUMBRIA, ENGLAND

2 0 1 6

THE FARAWAY NORTH

Published in 2016 by Northern Displayers, Skadi Press, England
www.northerndisplayers.co.uk

ISBN 978-0-9576120-2-0

Contents

CONTENTS

PREFACE

The so-called medieval ballads of Scandinavia seem to have come into fashion sometime around the 1300s — although a lack of documentary evidence makes precise and accurate dating impossible — and to have continued as a popular form of entertainment for several hundred years. The ballads are storytelling songs, and the stories they tell cover a wide range of subject matter. There are tales of heroes and trolls, romance, tragic death, and revenge, the supernatural creatures of folklore, and the miracles of saints. The ballads conjure images of the Scandinavian landscape — the desolate troll fells and heathlands of the north, the endless tracts of forest, and of course the seaways along the coast. I have chosen some fine examples for translation that I hope will bring these evocative ballads wider appreciation.

Swedish and Norwegian ballads have received rather less attention than their Danish counterparts in translation. For this book, I have used texts from all three of these countries, but Swedish and Norwegian ballads are well represented.

We begin with two classic Norwegian troll ballads, *Åsmund Frægdeg-jeva* and *Steinfinn Fefinnson*, and a troll ballad from Sweden in a similar style, *Esbjörn Proud and Orm the Strong*.

There are some Norwegian and Swedish romance ballads, some tragic, others with happier endings: *Bendik and Årolilja*, *Sunfair and the Dragon King*, *Sven Norman and Miss Gullborg*, *Little Lisa*, *Peter Pallebosson*, and *Sir*

Svedendal. This last ballad has a special place in the history of an Eddic poem.

I have included two takes on the ballad of the great hero Sigurd. The Danish (*Sivard Snare Sven*) and Norwegian (*Sigurd Sven*) ballads have a lot in common, but they are different enough that each stands as a separate ballad in its own right.

Some ballads with a particular significance in ballad history are included. A ballad fragment was used in lieu of placenames on a medieval map of Greenland. It is the first stanza of a ballad known in Swedish as *King Speleman*, which is included here. Late medieval ceiling paintings at Floda church in Sweden are some of the earliest representations of ballad action. And some of the ballads illustrated are included, with plenty of troll fighting: *Holger Dane and Burman* (from Swedish), *Sven Felding* (from Swedish and Danish), and *St Olaf's Saling Race* (from Danish).

Some further notes about the translation, Scandinavian names, and occasional obscure historical terms are given at the end of the book.

1   ÅSMUND FRÆGDEGJEVA

The ballad of *Åsmund Frægdegjeva* is a fine example of a classic Norwegian troll ballad. Our adventuring hero must travel away to the troll country of the north and fight with trolls to achieve his goal.

This ballad seems to be based on a legendary Norse saga about a man named Asmund Flagðagæfa. This old saga does not survive, but stories passed down orally based on the putative saga were written down in Iceland around 1700. It is interesting to see how Åsmund's name has changed between the Icelandic saga and the Norwegian ballad. The byname *Flagðagæfa* means "luck with the troll-woman"; the byname *Frægdegjeva* is apparently derived from this, but the word has changed such that it means something like "great and worthy". Indeed, much is made in the ballad of how "frægd" (i.e., great or renowned) Åsmund is: in the initial scene at the king's court, and again when he is talking to his brothers. So in the evolution of the name, this aspect of Åsmund's character is emphasised. In some versions of the ballad he is simply known as *frægde Åsmund* (i.e., great Åsmund).

A lot of action is packed into these ballad verses: Åsmund is sent away to the troll country of the north to rescue the King's sister. He takes his brothers with him, but they turn out to be rather less great than him. Åsmund leaves the ship and goes alone to the troll woman's vast halls in the high fells. He finds the girl there, but she is reluctant to be rescued at first, as she seems to have been bewitched into believing that the troll woman is her mother. When the troll woman appears, she tells Åsmund a story of how she visited the Christian country but couldn't stand to stay. Åsmund is able to kill the troll with red-hot iron, but he is betrayed by his cowardly brothers, who have fled with the ship.

The end of the ballad is remarkable. Åsmund escapes by riding across the sea — with the girl and plenty of gold — on the back of a magical horse. But then Åsmund beheads the horse, and it is transformed as a result into a man. Apparently, he had been bewitched, giving him the appearance of a horse, and the beheading broke the spell.

The troll woman in the ballad is called *Skome Gyvri*, which means the dark troll woman.

It was Ireland's king so bold,
   Was talking to his men:
"My sister is in Trollbotten,
   "Who'll fetch her back again?"
The day is never dawning

"Listen Åsmund Frejdegjæva,
   "To what I say to you:
"You'll go north to Trollbotten,
   "To fetch my sister home.

"Listen Åsmund Frejdegjæva,
   "The greatest man I know:
"You'll go north to Trollbotten,
   "To save my sister from woe."

"How I have I offended you,
   "O King, will you say,
"That you will send me off to the north,
   "To Trollbotten far away?"

"If you fetch my sister home,
  "And risk for her your life,
"I will make her your young bride,
  "She'd be so fair a wife."

"Well if you give me your sister,
  "Miss Ermeline fair and fine,
"Then I'll go north to the darkest land,
  "Where the sunlight never shines."

Åsmund took St Olof's ship,
  They called it Dragon the long.
They weighed the anchor and raised the sail,
  So the ship could come along.

They hoisted high the silken sail,
  Up to the gilded spar,
And it wasn't struck to the benches down,
  Till Trollbotten they saw.

And then they cast their anchor,
  Out on the whitest sand,
And it was Åsmund Frejdegjæva,
  The first who stepped to land.

What will you do, my brothers two?
  Will you guard my ship on the shore?
Or will you go into the mountains,
  To fetch out the maiden fair?

So answered Åsmund's brothers two,
  They were both young and shy:
"It seems that our great brother,
  "He wants us both to die."

"I'd rather, my great brother,
  "Guard the ship on the shore,
"I don't want to go to the mountains,
  "To fetch out the maiden fair."

So Åsmund came to the first hall,
  An awful view he surveyed,
The cloths there were all drenched in blood,
  And dragons at tables played.

And so he came to the second hall,
  A scene of sorrow and more:
Cauldrons were standing there on the ground,
  And small trolls oversaw.

And so he came to the third hall,
  And there was a prettier sight:
Fifteen beds stood all prepared,
  With silken sheets so white.

Fifteen beds stood all prepared,
  With white and silken sheets,
Åsmund leapt into one of them,
  And there he fell asleep.

In then came the maiden fair,
  Who Åsmund wanted to wed,
She had hair like fine-spun gold,
  Plaited with silken thread.

And in she came, the maiden fair,
  Who Åsmund wanted to win,
She had hair like fine-spun gold,
  With silk strands plaited in.

She had hair like fine-spun gold,
    Plaited with silken yarn,
And Åsmund sprang up out of his bed,
    And took her into his arms.

"Let me go now, Åsmund,
    "Don't hold me in your arms,
"When my mother comes in here,
    "She'll eat any Christian man!"

"You say that she's your mother,
    "As though you knew no better,
"But you are sister to Harald the King,
    "Who lives to the south of here."

In came Skome Gyvri,
    She grunted and she growled:
"Who is that for a spoilt brat,
    "Who dares the maid to hold?"

"If you call me a spoilt brat,
    "Suffering soon you'll see!
"They call me Åsmund Frejdegjæva,
    "And *that* you should call me!

"Listen Skome Gyvri,
    "To what I ask of you:
"How did you get that belt so broad,
    "You're wearing round you now?"

"Not last year but the year before,
    "I was on St Olof's estate,
"I thought that I would kill the King,
    "On Christmas night so late.

"I lifted him up upon my back,
    "I felt so young again,
"But when I came to the outer hall,
    "He felt too heavy then.

"Out then stepped the holy priest,
    "That man I couldn't stand.
"Holy water he splashed on me,
    "And still I can feel the sting.

"I felt that there in that land of theirs,
    "Peace I'd never know,
"So I tore the belt from the back of the King,
    "And crept to the earth below.

"Now listen Åsmund Frejdegjæva,
    "To what I say to you:
"Heat the iron glowing hot,
    "And send it here to me."

And it was Åsmund Frejdegjæva,
    He heated the iron fully,
And thrust it at Skome Gyvri,
    So the tip stuck into her belly.

And so spoke Skome Gyvri,
    As she fell dead to the ground:
"You'll not come out of this mountain alive,
    "Nor over the salty sound!"

And it was Åsmund Frejdegjæva,
    He went down to the strand,
But sailed and gone were his brothers two,
    No ship lay there on the land.

So Åsmund went to a fourth hall,
  No horrors did he behold,
But there he found a fleet-foot foal,
  Bound with bands of gold.

"Now listen, fairest fleet-foot foal,
  "What will you have from me,
"That you will run across the sound,
  "And hasten under me?

"How much of the reddest gold,
  "Will you have from me,
"If you, O fairest fleet-foot foal,
  "Carry me over the sea?"

"Not any of the reddest gold,
  "Will I take from you,
"But if you give me your right hand,
  "Then I'll run under you."

Answered Åsmund Frejdegjæva,
  As God advised him to:
"Yes I'll give you my right hand,
  "If you carry both of us two!"

"Listen up Miss Ermeline,
  "You gather up gold in store!
"And I will go to the drinking hall,
  "To play there with my sword."

And Åsmund came to a fifth hall,
  So angry in his mind,
He cut to pieces the ring-tables,
  They rattled in every ring.

He cut down all the small trolls,
　　Before his eyes he saw,
And when he came out of Trollbotten,
　　It flowed with blood and gore.

And so they took both silver and gold,
　　As much as they could find,
And set it all on the horse's back,
　　Over the sea to ride.

And it was the fairest fleet-foot foal,
　　So quickly he did bound,
They rode across the water wide,
　　As though it was solid ground.

The King he stood in the high loft,
　　And he looked out so wide:
"Now I see Åsmund Frejdegjæva,
　　"Across the sea he rides!"

And it was Åsmund Frejdegjæva,
　　He stepped on the whitest sand,
He cut off the head of the fleet-foot foal,
　　It became a Christian man.
The day is never dawning

ÅSMUND FRÆGDEGJEVA

2 | STEINFINN FEFINNSON

The ballad of *Steinfinn Fefinnson* is a second troll ballad from Norway. It begins one winter's night when a visitor comes knocking on a farmhouse door carrying fresh animal skins that he has hunted. It transpires that the wanderer is our hero, Steinfinn Fefinnson, out searching for his sisters, who have been stolen away by a troll.

The local farmer is able to advise Steinfinn how he might find the troll up on the heath. When Steinfinn puts the farmer's plan into action, he is able to dispatch the troll mother with little problem. But no matter how many trolls he manages to shoot, more just keep on coming, so it turns out to be rather important for Steinfinn that trolls are turned to stone in sunlight.

The horse's name, *Soten*, means Sooty or Blacky. Again, *Gyvri* is the troll, and here *Skome Heath* means the dark heath.

It was Steinfinn Fefinnson,
    He came so late one night:
"Farmer will you give me shelter?
"My pelts I need to dry."
Here nobody wants to go dancing!

"Yes I'll house you for the night,
  "And here your pelts you can dry,
"But if you know of any news,
  "Then this you'll tell to me!"

"Stolen away are my sisters two,
  "No clearer can I speak.
"But it's been said to me in truth:
  "They're up on Skome Heath."

"Skome Heath I know so well,
  "Every bush around.
"If I were as good with a bow as you,
  "They'd surely soon be found!

"Listen Steinfinn Fefinnson:
  "Go to the stony tor.
"To the south you'll have the wilderness,
  "To the north you'll have the moor.

"And listen Steinfinn Fefinnson:
  "Lie by your horse's neck.
"Soten will neigh when she sees the troll,
  "And then will Steinfinn wake!"

It was Steinfinn Fefinnson,
  He went to the stony tor.
To the south there lay the wilderness,
  To the north there lay the moor.

And it was Steinfinn Fefinnson,
  He lay by his horse's neck.
Soten neighed when she saw the troll,
  And then did Steinfinn wake!

Out then came the troll mother,
　　She wanted to blow on the steak,
And Steinfinn smiled and thought to himself:
　　"Right on time you came!"

And out then came the troll mother,
　　She wanted to cut her share,
And Steinfinn smiled and thought to himself:
　　"Now you just wait right there!"

And it was Steinfinn Fefinnson,
　　He shot his arrows wide,
He shot the old troll mother,
　　So her hair came into her eyes.

It was Steinfinn Fefinnson,
　　He let his arrows fly,
And so the old troll mother thought,
　　That hail fell down from the sky:

"It's cold up here on Skome Heath,
　　"When the wind from the sea does blow.
"Sharp are all these giants' teeth,
　　"That gust from the drifted snow."

It was Steinfinn Fefinnson,
　　He took an arrow bright,
And so he shot the troll mother,
　　So the tip it stood in her heart.

It was Steinfinn Fefinnson,
　　Was shooting more and more,
And so he shot the troll mother,
　　So she had to sink to the floor.

Out came all the small trolls,
    A game they thought they played:
"What do you think is wrong with mother?
    "Her jaws are open wide."

And it was all the small trolls,
    Such horror they did feel:
"What do you think is wrong with mother?
    "She's kicking so hard with her heels."

So many were the small trolls,
    Round every bush they crawled,
Steinfinn had not fewer,
    Than fifteen with each shot.

And it was Steinfinn Fefinnson,
    With shooting he grew tired:
"Do you think that over Skome Heath,
    "The clear sun soon will rise?"

It was Steinfinn Fefinnson,
    He looked to the mountain high:
"They're taking away that maiden fair,
    "She runs on feet so fine."

So far ran the small trolls,
    With the maiden they tried to go,
But then they turned to granite stones,
    That stand in the valley below.

So far ran the small trolls,
    The sun it shone in their eyes,
And so they turned to granite stones,
    That stand there, up on the rise.
Here nobody wants to go dancing!

15

3 | ESBJÖRN PROUD AND ORM THE STRONG

The Swedish ballad of *Esbjörn Proud and Orm the Strong* has a similar theme to the Norwegian troll ballads. The story it tells is also told in the short Icelandic saga *Orms þattr Storolfssonar*, and in the Faeroese ballad *Brusajøkils Kvad*. Orm Storolfsson was a famous figure in Iceland with legendary strength. He is mentioned in several sagas as Orm the Strong, including *Gretti's saga*, *Njal's saga*, and *Egil's saga*.

The ballad tells of how one winter's night, a visitor knocks on the door of Esbjörn and Orm, looking for shelter, and telling stories of gold in the faraway troll country. They let him stay the night, but when he leaves in the morning without giving them any of the gold he promised them, Esbjörn is not pleased. So Esbjörn sails away to the troll country, and he meets his death at the hands (or in the mouth) of a monstrous cat. Orm has sworn to avenge his brother, so when he learns of his death, he decides to sail, but first prays to St Erik that he will be successful.

Orm arrives in the troll country, manages to slay the cat, and almost sets sail again for home. He realises, though, that he has forgotten his gloves back up at the troll's hall. He has to go back for the gloves. But there he meets the troll who visited them that winter's night. They fight, and things don't go well for the troll.

The troll is called *Bruse* (meaning "rough" or "gruff"), and the troll country is called *Trollewalk*. The presence of the cat is not explained in the Swedish ballad, but in the Icelandic þattr, it is told that the cat is the troll's mother.

There is another rather similar Swedish ballad called *Ulf the Strong*. In that ballad, Ulf also goes to the troll country (called *Gigerhall*), fights unsuccessfully with a troll (called *Faxe*), and asks his brother (also called Orm the Strong) to avenge his death.

Esbjörn Proud and Orm the Strong,
　　Were drinking in the hall,
And so there came a wanderer,
　　Late one night at Yule.
So wide they set up tents in Issland

"Sit in peace, Esbjörn Proud,
　　"Across the table broad.
"If you house me for the night,
　　"Then you're a fighter good!"

"Shelter I will give tonight,
　　"Wanderer, to you,
"But if you have some reddest gold,
　　"This to me you'll show!"

"Yes I have more reddest gold,
　　"Than fifteen kings possess.
"But a man won't live for very long,
　　"When for gold he asks."

"Listen up, good wanderer,
　　"If you've lied to me,
"Then I shall hang you up so high,
　　"In the gallows tree."

"I have never learned to lie,
   "Since I was in my youth,
"And if you come to Trollewalk,
   "You'll see I speak the truth."

'Twas early in the morning,
   When they rose out of bed,
They understood the treachery:
   The wanderer had fled.

It was fighter Esbjörn Proud,
   Was playing with his knife:
"I'll go and visit Bruse strong,
   "Though it may cost my life."

"Listen, fighter Orm the Strong,
   "To me will you be true?
"Say, will you avenge my death,
   "As we are Christians two?"

"Long ago I promised you,
   "I promise now again:
"Yes, I will avenge your death,
   "As we are Christian men!"

It was fighter Esbjörn Proud,
   He set out from the land,
He hoisted high his silken sail,
   And sailed to Bruse's strand.

He sailed across the salty sea,
   Away to Bruse's strand,
And it was fighter Esbjörn Proud,
   The first to step to land.

19

And so he set out all his men,
Around the table there,
And in the middle, Esbjörn Proud,
Sat in Bruse's chair.

The time drew on to evening,
The cat came prowling in,
And she took fighter Esbjörn Proud,
And rushed away with him.

Orm he lived in the mountain,
And life was good as ever,
But fewer cares he would have had,
If he didn't have a brother.

But thanks to fighter Orm the Strong,
The news he did discover.
He never could be called a man,
Who didn't avenge his brother.

"Now grant me this, St Erik,
"The gold I may bring home,
"And half of all that reddest gold,
"I will send to Rome!"

'Twas Wednesday in the evening,
His ship was rigged to sail,
And so he sailed to Issland in,
Late that very day.

He hoisted high the silken sail,
And sailed to Bruse's strand,
And it was fighter Orm the Strong,
The first who stepped to land.

And so he set out all his men,
　　Around the table there,
And in the middle, their youngest man,
　　Sat in Bruse's chair.

And so he set out all his men,
　　Like Esbjörn Proud before,
And close beside them, Orm the Strong,
　　Sat by Bruse's door.

The time drew on to evening,
　　The cat came prowling in,
And so she took their youngest man,
　　And tried to flee with him.

Orm he struck with his gilded spear,
　　The sulphur smoked and blew.
The cat it clamped its teeth together,
　　And bit the man in two.

Then came fifteen thurs-trolls,
　　With fire burning bright:
"Listen up, Orm the Strong,
　　"It will be warm tonight!"

Orm went down to the green sea-strand,
　　He meant to leave for home.
He found he'd left his gloves behind,
　　They lay upon a stone.

Then the steersman shouted out,
　　Up in the prow he was standing:
"I think that other gloves you'll find,
　　"When back at home we're landing."

"Never will the ladies tell,
  "Back in our land at home,
"Of how I left my gloves behind,
  "For ugly Bruse to own."

And so he went back up again,
  His gloves he thought he'd find,
But he met ugly Bruse there,
  It was an awful sight.

They fought together with their hands,
  The fighters gave their all:
"Say are you not that ugly thief,
  "Who stayed with me last Yule?

"Horses' hay and goats' hair,
  "Are hanging in your belly,
"You have nails like goats' horns,
  "On every finger many!

"And I can see there in your eyes,
  "Floating islands two,
"I say my eyes have never seen,
  "An uglier troll than you!"

They fought together with their hands,
  They came together with rage.
The mountain flowed beneath their feet,
  That they had crushed to clay.

They fought together a second fight,
  There flew both flesh and blood.
The mountain flowed beneath their feet,
  That they had trod to mud.

"Listen up, Orm the Strong,
"If you let me live,
"Half of all my reddest gold,
"To you I'll gladly give."

And so it was old Bruse,
He raised a slab of stone:
"Step down, fighter Orm the Strong,
"And take from all the gold."

"Listen up, you ugly troll,
"Your tricks I understand!
"If I get any gold from you,
"You'll put it in my hand."

And so it was old Bruse,
Into the pit he stepped,
And it was fighter Orm the Strong,
At that, cut off his head.

Now they've been in Bruse's land,
And they've won honour there,
They loaded ships with reddest gold,
As much as they could bear.

Thanks to fighter Orm the Strong,
So well his word he kept,
And half of all the reddest gold,
Away to Rome he sent.
So wide they set up tents in Issland

ESBJÖRN PROUD AND ORM THE STRONG

4 | SUNFAIR AND THE DRAGON KING

The ballad of *Sunfair and the Dragon King* has a certain fame because it was used by Grieg (*Solfager og Ormekongen*) in his *Norwegian Folk Songs and Folk Dances*.

The ballad itself tells a rather gruesome story: when Sunfair refuses to run away with the Dragon King, first he drugs her, then he buries her alive, and then he asks her whether she will reconsider. She soon comes around.

But Sunfair's husband Sir David had marked her hand so that he would always be able to recognise her, and when he hears where she might be from a wandering traveller, he disguises himself as a pilgrim, and leaves to try to find her. As it happens, she is easily identified as she is incongruously wearing gloves — obviously with the intention of hiding a mark on her hand. Sir David has to deal with the Dragon King before they can return home.

> Miss Sunfair she was so fair a maid,
> *While the maiden was so young*
> That there was none fairer in that place.
> *I want to ride out in the woodland*

27

Miss Sunfair she was so fair a wife,
    That the danger was great for Sir David's life.

He marked a gold cross on Miss Sunfair's hand,
    So she could be found in a faraway land.

The Dragon King came riding into the yard,
    Miss Sunfair was standing and sunning her hair.

And the Dragon King spoke to Miss Sunfair so:
    "Do you have for your head a crown of gold?"

"Crowns of gold I have five and ten,
    "And Sir David has given me all of them."

"Listen Miss Sunfair, and hear what I say:
    "Abandon Sir David, be married with me."

"No, that will never happen I fear,
    "For Sir David is held in my heart so dear."

So the Dragon King gave her a sleeping drink good,
    And Miss Sunfair she fainted, there where she stood.

The Dragon King gave her two sleeping drinks more,
    And Miss Sunfair she fainted and sank to the floor.

And the message came soon to Sir David's door:
    "Miss Sunfair is dead, all-dearest of yours."

They laid Miss Sunfair out on a bier,
    And Sir David he rode so sorrowfully there.

They buried her under the mud and the stone,
    And Sir David he rode so sorrowfully home.

Late in the evening the moon shone clear,
    And the Dragon King rode to the churchyard there.

"Would you rather live lying there under a stone,
  "Or would you follow the Dragon King home?"

"I cannot live lying here under a stone,
  "Rather I'd follow the Dragon King home."

"Would you rather live lying there under the clay,
  "Or would you live as the Dragon King's maid?"

"I cannot live lying here under the clay,
  "Rather I'd live as the Dragon King's maid."

They lifted Miss Sunfair up out of the ground,
  And carried her off, away from the land.

And so there appeared an old wandering man,
  Who knew all the news from faraway lands.

"Sir David, this is so dreadful to tell:
  "Miss Sunfair she lives in a golden hall.

"Now you should cut yourself pilgrims' clothes,
  "Then away like a pilgrim you can go.

"Take your pilgrims' staff in your hand,
  "And wander away to the Dragon King's land."

Sir David he came walking into the yard,
  Miss Sunfair was standing and sunning her hair.

"Listen Miss Sunfair, what I ask of you:
  "Say, can you give me shelter and food?"

"If you go into the lodging house,
  "Food for you I'll gladly bring out."

And all that she gave, and all that she bore,
  Always gloves on her hands she wore.

"And is it the custom, here in this land,
    "Not to break bread with your bare hands?"

"I don't believe you're a wandering man,
    "So I should break bread with gloves on my hands."

"I may not be now but I was at that time,
    "When I gave a gold crown to that fast-maid of mine.

"I may not be now but I was in the days,
    "When there in my arms Miss Sunfair lay."

Miss Sunfair she lifted the pilgrim's hat:
    "If you're Sir David then tell me that!"

"Listen Miss Sunfair, what I ask of you:
    "Will you come back to our home with me?"

"Yes I'd come back to our home with you,
    "If I knew that the Dragon King couldn't see me."

Sir David he went to the lodging-house in,
    With his sword held under a scarlet skin.

Sir David he lifted his sword so sharp,
    And he cut the Dragon King into two halves.

Sir David had a horse so calm and so kind,
    And he rode with Miss Sunfair sitting behind.

And so they rode home to Sir David's land,
    While the maiden was so young
Like the sun that over the felltops ran.
    I want to ride out in the woodland

31

SUNFAIR AND THE DRAGON KING

5 | BENDIK AND ÅROLILJA

The ballad singer makes no secret of the inevitability of Bendik's down-
fall. Even in the opening stanza of the ballad, as our hero rides away to
look for a wife, we hear that it will be impossible for him to return, and
that he must die. The ballad of *Bendik and Årolilja* is a classic Norwegian
ballad of the tragedy of forbidden love.

> Bendik rode to Selando,
>   He went to find a wife,
> It was his fate that he'd never return,
>   And so he lost his life.
> *Årolilja, why do you sleep so long?*
>
> Bendik rode to Selando,
>   A maid he went to find,
> It was his fate that he'd never return,
>   And so he had to die.
>
> He hadn't been in the court of the king,
>   As many weeks as eight,
> And then he fell for the daughter of the king,
>   In a love so great.

The king he built a golden track,
  It was both steep and wide:
"He who treads on the golden track,
  "Trouble he'll surely find!"

The king he built a golden track,
  It was both steep and high:
"He who treads on the golden track,
  "He'll surely lose his life!"

Answered then young Bendik,
  He was standing close at hand:
"I dare tread on the golden track,
  "Against the King's command!

Bendik rode in the woods by day,
  To hunt the hart and hind,
By night he slept with his maiden fair,
  All under the linen fine.

Bendik rode in the woods by day,
  To hunt the wild roe deer,
By night he slept with his maiden fair,
  The price he'd pay was dear.

"When I sit with you, it seems
  "I sit in sunshine bright.
"When you and I are together,
  "Both mind and heart are light."

"When I sit with you, it seems
  "I sit in sunshine warm.
"When you and I have to part,
  "Both heart and mind are torn."

34

"So fond I am of your yellow hair,
    "Like apples on the branches.
"Happy is he who may have you,
    "God help the one who misses!"

In then came the king's small boy,
    In with the news he ran:
"Bendik treads on the golden track,
    "Against the king's command!"

And so it was the Danish king,
    He struck the table hard:
"No longer will Bendik live his life,
    "By all that's in the world!

"At Lund's church in Skåne,
    "The roof is covered with gold,
"No longer will Bendik live his life,
    "Even if it was three times filled.

"At Lund's church in Skåne,
    "The roof is covered with lead,
"No longer will Bendik live his life,
    "Even if it was newly raised."

And so they took young Bendik,
    And threw him on the ground,
And fifteen were the bast-ropes,
    With which his feet were bound.

Fifteen were the bast-ropes,
    With which his feet were tied.
But those he broke and tore apart,
    Like they were made of thread.

In then came the king's small boy,
  The news in the yard he'd spoken:
"Take one of Årolilja's hairs,
  "And a prisoner he'll be taken."

So they took one of Årolilja's hairs,
  And bound young Bendik's hands.
"Rather than tear this apart,
  "I'll stay here in these bonds."

And so they set young Bendik,
  In the prison hall,
And Årolilja's salty tears,
  Ran down her cheeks so pale.

They prayed for him young Bendik,
  All those who had speech,
The birds that sat on the branches high,
  And the deer that ran beneath.

They prayed for him young Bendik,
  All those who had life,
The trees that stood in the wildest wood,
  And the flowers that grew on the heights.

They prayed for him young Bendik,
  All those who could pray,
The men who lived in this world of men,
  And the fish in the deepest sea.

And in came Årolilja,
  She fell down on her knees:
"Listen up, O father dear:
  "You give the prisoner to me!"

"Leave me Årolilja,
    "I will not hear a word!
"It would be bad if women's blood,
    "Should redden my good sword."

In then came the Danish queen,
    Tears ran on her cheeks:
"I beg you dearest lord of mine,
    "To grant me what I seek:

"You took me from my father's yard,
    "Against my father's word,
"Saying anything I ask of you,
    "I always will be heard."

"And anything you ask of me,
    "I always will consent.
"Except that Bendik will live his life,
    "And this you'll never get."

By the church's southern side,
    There did Bendik die,
And high up in the high loft,
    She broke, his own fair maid.

By the church's southern side,
    There Bendik lost his life,
And high up in the high loft,
    She broke, his own dear wife.

In then came the king's small boy,
    The news he spoke aloud:
"Årolilja is lying dead,
    "All under the burial shroud!"

37

"Had I known this yesterday,
  "So much their love was worth,
"Bendik wouldn't have lost his life,
  "For all that's on the earth!"

They laid young Bendik in the south,
  And Årolilja in the north,
And so there grew upon their graves,
  Two lily flowers forth.

And so there grew upon their graves,
  Two lily bushes fine,
They wound together above the church,
  And they bring the king such pain.

And so there grew upon their graves,
  Two lily bushes fair,
They wound together above the church,
  And they bring the king despair.
Årolilja, why do you sleep so long?

BENDIK AND ÅROLILJA

6 SIGURD SVEN

Sigurd the dragon killer is one of the greatest and most renowned of all the Germanic heroes. His story is told in the Norse *Volsungasaga*, and also in parts of the poetic and prose Eddas. But there is more than one version of the Sigurd legend. It is told in different forms in the Norse *Didrikssaga*, and in the German *Song of the Nibelungs* (where he is called Siegfried).

Sigurd also appears in several Scandinavian ballads, often as *Sivard Snare Sven* (where *Snare* means quick), and often in those ballads that deal with Diderick of Bern. For example, he is mentioned in *Widrick Waylandsson's Fight with Long Ben Reyser*, and he plays a major part in the action in *Twelve Strong Fighters* (both translated in *Warrior Lore*).

But Sigurd also has his own signature ballads. Two rather different stories of Sigurd are translated and included here: a version from Danish and one from Norwegian tradition. Both ballads are about a journey made by Sigurd on a great grey horse given to him by his mother with a warning to take care. Although the two ballads do have a lot in common, the stories are also different enough that it is interesting to present both.

Readers with some knowledge of Norse legends may find the names that appear in the Norwegian ballad of *Sigurd Sven* familiar. Sigurd's grey horse is called *Grane* (*cf Grani* in *Volsungasaga*), and his uncle is

41

called *Greive* (*cf Grip* in *Volsungasaga*). One of Sigurd's women also makes an appearance: *Guro Rysserova* is Gudrun. The epithet *Rysserova* means horse-tail. Thus in Norwegian folklore, Gudrun has become like a supernatural Huldra creature, who commonly appear with animals' tails. *Rinarfoss* is the name of a waterfall on the River Rhine, which might be translated as the Rhine Falls, Rhine Force, or Rhine Foss on the basis of waterfall names in different parts of England. Sigurd's mother is named *Grindill* in this ballad.

The Norwegian ballad seems to be related to a particular journey made by Sigurd as told in *Volsungasaga*, and in *Gripisspå* in the Poetic Edda. In that story, Sigurd makes the journey to visit his uncle Grip, a seer, who tells him that he must avenge the death of his father. In the ballad, the story is somewhat different: Sigurd goes to visit his uncle Greive to try to find information about his unknown father.

In the ballad, both Sigurd and his horse are depicted as big and aggressive. The uncle says that Sigurd will not tolerate any insults, and in the opening scene of the ballad, we see how he responds to the taunts of his playmates on the playing field with violence. On the journey, Sigurd meets an oversized troll, and Grane has no trouble carrying both the troll and Sigurd. The horse also terrorises the other horses in the stable while Sigurd is speaking to his uncle.

But the journey is unsuccessful. Sigurd's uncle does not tell him who is father is, and moreover he tells him that he is dead. Sigurd is paid off with a chest of gold, but things continue to go wrong as Sigurd rides away.

The *Oskorei* (the thunder ride; also sometimes known as *Åsgardsrei*, the Asgard ride) is the Norwegian name for the Wild Hunt. According to folklore, the Oskorei is a wild group of dead souls who ride on horseback through the night. It is not a good thing to meet the Wild Hunt as they ride out, so Sigurd naturally tries to ride away when he first sees them. In Norwegian tradition, Sigurd is the leader of the Wild Hunt, and Guro Rysserova is another of the riders. So this ballad can also be seen as telling the story of how Sigurd came to lead the Oskorei.

It was the king's small boys,
   They wandered all so wide,
And out they went to the playing field,
   And in a ring they played.

Sigurd he went to the playing field,
   He knocked a small boy down,
He struck at one of them under the ear,
   They laughed at him so loud.

Sigurd he was tall and strong,
   He didn't play for fun.
And soon the king's small boys were sore,
   And blood on the field did run.

And so they spoke, the small boys,
   Angry as they were:
"Better you find out your father's name,
   "Than make us suffer sore."

Sigurd he threw the playing ball,
   No more he wanted to play,
And in he went to his mother dear,
   He made her cheeks go pale.

And it was then Sigurd Sven,
   He set on his shoulders a a skin,
And up he went to the high loft,
   To his dearest mother in.

"Listen up, O mother dear:
   "Free me from my pain,
"Tell me now my father's name,
   "It's hard to live in shame."

"Listen, dearest son of mine:
    "I won't encourage you,
"But go to Greive, your uncle,
    "And he will counsel you."

"Well you know, my mother dear,
    "My way there will be long,
"How will I travel away from here,
    "Will I walk or ride along?"

"There stands a horse in the stable-house,
    "The small boys call him Grane,
"He will take you away from here,
    "And he will carry you far.

"There stands a horse in the stable-house,
    "The small boys call him Grane,
"But watch yourself, O son of mine,
    "Or he will be your ruin."

"Listen up, O mother dear:
    "Don't you sorrow or cry,
"My childhood I have left behind,
    "My horse I've learned to ride!"

Grindill she went to the stable-house,
    Loosed Grane from his bonds,
And Sigurd he stood in the stable gloom,
    And took him with his hands.

Sigurd he laid on the gilded saddle,
    And tight he tied the girth,
"Today the boys won't laugh at me,
    "For Grane will gallop forth!"

And Sigurd he tied the gilded bridle,
　　Over the horse's mane:
"Either I will steer you today,
　　"Or die hanging onto the reins."

Grindill she went into the house,
　　She mixed up mead and wine,
And she sent it then to her dearest son,
　　Where he sat on his horse so high.

Sigurd he rode away from the house,
　　With shield and armour bright,
His mother she followed him far from the town,
　　So mild is a mother's heart.

And it was then Sigurd Sven,
　　He rode on under the hills,
And a troll came down from the high fells,
　　And asked to ride with him.

A troll came down from the high fells,
　　All dressed in a shirt of silk,
His nose was like a cattleshed,
　　And his eyes like tarns on the hill.

The troll came down from the high fells,
　　All dressed in a shirt so white:
"Now listen up, O Sigurd Sven:
　　"With you I want to ride!"

"Climb up onto the end of the cloth,
　　"Both of us Grane will bear,
"And I will hold the reins myself,
　　"And take my chances there."

Fifteen ells were Grane's legs,
    To his hooves right down,
The troll he rode on Grane's back,
    And his feet they dragged on the ground.

The troll he rode so very long,
    That Sigurd was dismayed,
Then Grane shook the troll off,
    All so his back did break.

And not a house did Sigurd see,
    As he rode all through the day,
Until he came to Bortingsborg,
    Where Greive's castle lay.

And Greive the king he spoke so,
    As he sat at dinner time:
"Now I hear that someone
    "Outside the castle rides."

Mead they drank from silver bowls,
    That always were refilled:
"Here comes Sigurd, my sister's son.
    "He's visiting here in the hills."

And mead they drank from silver bowls,
    And treated each other right:
"It is Sigurd, my sister's son,
    "He'll not take any slight."

"Grane will go to the stable-house,
    "And eat the oats and hay,
"And Sigurd will go to the high loft,
    "And drink with ladies and maids."

"Grane will go to the stable-house,
  "And eat the oats and corn,
"And Sigurd will go to the high loft,
  "To drink from a silver horn."

And Grane they led to the stable-house,
  The small boys called him tall!
And then he forced all Greive's horses
  Over to one of the walls.

Grane he stood in the stable-house,
  He raised his voice so loud.
Some he hit so they broke their necks,
  Some lost teeth from their mouths.

"Listen up, O uncle of mine,
  "To what I ask of you:
"What do you know of my father?
  "Don't hide it from me now."

"Nothing I know of your father,
  "I live in the hills so high,
"But I have long believed it true,
  "That under a stone he lies."

And it was then Sigurd Sven,
  He drew his sword from its sheath:
"If you don't tell me my father's name,
  "Then it will be your death!"

"You be quiet, Sigurd Sven,
  "And put your sword away,
"I will give you silver and gold,
  "As much as you can take.

"I'll give to you a chest of gold,
   "Made in Bjarmeland.
"Go home now back to your mother,
   "And carry yourself like a man."

"I will ride away from here,
   "In scandal and in shame,
"And never I'll see the land of my birth,
   "Nor my mother again."

Sigurd he rode from Greive's house,
   So angry in his mind,
But when he came to the darkest woods,
   He met the Oskorei.

And Guro Rysserov' took her harp,
   And Gunnar he played a note,
And Sigurd he rode to Rinarfoss,
   But Grane broke his foot.

Sigurd he rode in Rinarfoss,
   And Grane broke his foot,
And Sigurd he dropped the golden chest,
   And then the gold was lost.

Sigurd he held the golden ring,
   The chest it fell in the stream,
"Surely Grane's bewitched by Guro,
   "He pulls so hard on the reins."

Sigurd he held the golden ring,
   The chest it floated away,
And fifteen were the waterfalls,
   That Grane leapt that day.

"Listen then, O Sigurd Sven,
   "To the choice that you'll be given:
"Would you rather lead the Oskorei,
   "Or be the lowest in heaven?"

"Well, listen Guro Rysserov':
   "It isn't hard to choose,
"But if Grane hadn't broken his foot,
   "I'd have ridden away from you.

"I'll ride with you to Asgard then,
   "If Grane can carry me,
"And I will lead the Oskorei,
   "A vassal's no good to be."

"Grane is so weak in his leg,
   "With us he cannot come,
"I'll lend you Skærting, my black horse,
   "And I will ride on a broom."

7   SIVARD SNARE SVEN

Following on from the Norwegian ballad of *Sigurd Sven*, the Danish ballad presented here gives an alternative take on the story. In the Danish ballad, our hero is called *Sivard Snare Sven*. The name of the horse in the ballad texts is *Gråmen* or similar, which I have rendered here as *Greyman*. The uncle is not named.

Unlike the Norwegian, the Danish ballad has no mention of the Oskorei, the conversation with the uncle, the meeting with the troll *en route*, or the initial argument with the young playmates. The story told in the Danish ballad focusses mainly on the gift of a horse for the journey, the wild nature of the horse, and the final leap over the wall into the uncle's castle yard. The reason for the journey is different again. We learn in the first stanza of this ballad that Sivard has killed his stepfather. Sigurd does kill his fosterfather in both *Volsungasaga* and *Didrikssaga* versions of the legend, though not necessarily before going to visit his uncle.

> Sivard he struck his stepfather down,
> All for his mother's best,
> And Sivard he longed to ride to court,
> His manhood he would test.
> *So happily runs Greyman under Sivard*

Sivard he went to his mother to stand,
  He spoke to his mother so:
"Will I have a horse to ride from here?
  "Or walking will I go?"

"No, you'll not walk away from here,
  "On horseback you'll be taken.
"I'll give to you a horse so good,
  "The one the boys call Greyman."

They led out Greyman from the stall,
  His bridle was of gold,
His eyes were bright as shining stars,
  And fire sprang from his nose.

Sivard he sat on Greyman's back,
  And full well could he ride,
And Greyman thought it was curious,
  To feel the spurs in his side.

And it was Sivard's mother dear,
  She followed him over the heath:
"You watch yourself, dear son of mine,
  "Watch out for Greyman's wrath."

"Listen up, O mother dear,
  "Don't you sorrow or cry,
"I have lived here long enough:
  "My horse I've learned to ride!"

It was Sivard Snare Sven,
  His horse he spurred on hard,
He rode three leaps out into the land,
  But things were not so good.

He rode three leaps out into the land,
    And things were not so good,
And this I say to you in truth:
    He sweated tears of blood.

For fifteen nights and fifteen days,
    He rode over hills and dales,
And so he came to a house so high,
    The gates were locked and sealed.

The king he stood in the high loft,
    And he looked out so wide:
"And here I see a drunken man,
    "Who well his horse can ride."

"That is not a drunken man,
    "Who well his horse can ride,
"Rather it's Sivard my sister's son,
    "From war he comes besides!"

The king he spoke to all his men:
    "I'll give you this advice:
"If that's Sivard Snare Sven,
    "He'll not take any slight."

And it was Sivard Snare Sven,
    His horse he spurred on hard,
And this I say to you in truth:
    He leapt into the yard.

Fifteen were the watchmen,
    Who guarded wall and tower,
But no man there knew anything,
    Till horse and man were over.
So happily runs Greyman under Sivard

8   LITTLE LISA

This tragic ballad was widespread throughout Scandinavia. When Lisa's mother discovers that her daughter is pregnant, she is not pleased, and vows to punish both Lisa and the man, a Sir Redevall. So Redevall and Lisa run away together. When they are out in the woods, Lisa gives birth to twin sons. But when Redevall goes to fetch water, he hears a nightingale by the brook sweetly singing its fateful song.

> Little Lisa and her mother they sat in the hall,
>   And together they had such a curious talk.
> *Ho ho, no no, no no!*

> The mother she spoke to her daughter so:
>   "Why is there running milk from your breast?"

> "It is not milk, though you thought it right,
>   "But it is the mead I was drinking last night."

> "So little are these two things alike,
>   "For mead it is brown, and milk it is white!"

> "No longer the truth can I hide from you,
>   "Sir Redevall he has tempted me."

"If Sir Redevall he has tempted you,
　"No more will I be a mother to you.

"Sir Redevall will I hang from a tree,
　"And you so will I roast on a spit."

Little Lisa she went to Sir Redevall's hall,
　And she knocked on the door with her fingers so small.

"Get up, Sir Redevall, let me come in!
　"For now I have spoken with dear mother mine.

"And listen, Sir Redevall, hear what I say:
　"My mother she is so angry with me.

"And you she wants to hang from a tree,
　"And me she wants to roast on a spit."

"Well never will I be hanged for you,
　"And never will you be burned for me."

Sir Redevall saddled his palfrey grey,
　He lifted her up and they rode away.

And when they came to the rosy grove,
　Little Lisa she wanted to rest for a while.

Sir Redevall spread out his cape so blue,
　And there little Lisa bore twin sons, two.

"I know of a stream that runs close by,
　"Will you now bring fresh water to me?"

But when he came to the stream where it ran,
　Sir Redevall heard how the nightingale sang.

So sweetly the nightingale sang overhead,
　It sang of little Lisa and her sons lying dead.

When Sir Redevall came to the rosy grove,
    He found it was true what the nightingale sang.

So he dug a grave both deep and wide,
    And there the bodies three he laid.

And Sir Redevall set his sword to a root,
    And the point against his heart he put.
Ho ho, no no, no no!

9 SVEN NORMAN AND MISS GULLBORG

The murder ballad story goes all wrong for serial killer Sven Norman
when he meets Miss Gullborg. He is able to lure her away from her
home with promises of a better life with him in a faraway land. But
when he shows her the grave he has dug that is just the right size for
her, Miss Gullborg comes up with a plan to survive.

Sven Norman he came riding into the yard,
    Miss Gullborg was standing and sunning her hair.
There he proposes
    Sven Norman lies deep under the mountain

"You don't have to let out your hair for me,
    "I didn't come to propose to you."

"Whether or not you came to propose,
    "I'd just as surely tell you 'no'."

"Listen Miss Gullborg, and hear what I say:
    "Will you come back to my land with me?

"I will take you away to a land,
    "Where you'll walk on gold as you walk here on sand.

"And I will take you away to a scene,
  "Where you'll live free of sorrow and die free of sin.

"Nothing else runs in the streams but wine,
  "And nothing else grows but linen fine.

"No other birds but cuckoos call,
  "And nothing else grows but onions small."

"If this is the truth you tell to me,
  "Then I'll come away to that land with you."

Miss Gullborg she gathered her gold in her case,
  Sven Norman he saddled his horse in haste.

Sven Norman's horse was so kind and so good,
  And there on his back Miss Gullborg she rode.

And when they came to the rosy grove,
  Sven Norman he wanted to rest for a while.

"Listen Sven Norman, what I ask of you:
  "Why are you digging a grave so new?"

"For my horse it's just a little too tight,
  "But for you, my dearest, it fits just right.

"Fifteen maidens now I've had,
  "And all of them into the grave I've laid."

"Fifteen knights have courted me,
  "And all of them I've deloused but you."

"Of course you can delouse my hair,
  "But while I sleep don't kill me there!"

Sven Norman he lay by Miss Gullborg's knee,
  And there he slept so long and so deep.

Miss Gullborg she took up her red gold bands,
    And she bound Sven Norman's snow-white hands.

Miss Gullborg she took up a red gold tether,
    And she bound Sven Norman's feet together.

"Wake up, Sven Norman, don't slumber so deep,
    "I swore not to kill you while you were asleep."

Sven Norman he woke and he looked around,
    He saw that from top to toe he was bound.

Miss Gullborg she took up her silver-blade knife,
    And she thrust it into Sven Norman's life.

"Sven Norman is lying for hawks and for ravens,
    "And still I have my maiden's name.

"Sven Norman is lying and floating in blood,
    "And still I am a maiden good."
There he proposes
    Sven Norman lies deep under the mountain

SVEN NORMAN AND MISS GULLBORG

PETER PALLEBOSSON

Peter Pallebosson dresses up in his finest clothes for a mission from which he will not be deterred, despite the warnings of his uncle and the misgivings of his sisters. He wants to win a wife. But unfortunately the girl in question is the daughter of the Danish king, she is engaged to be married to someone else, and she is on her way to the cathedral church in Lund for the wedding.

Peter does escape with the girl, little Kerstin. And she goes with him willingly. But the Danish king and her fiance Nils are in pursuit.

This ballad is translated from the Swedish. Although Lund, Skåne, and Halland are all now in Sweden, until 1658 they were part of Denmark, which could explain the references to Denmark in the ballad text.

> 'Twas early in the morning,
>   The lark was singing sweetly,
> Up stood Peter Pallebosson,
>   He dressed himself so neatly.
> *You're riding out!*
>
> All in silk he dressed himself,
>   And also noble furs,
> And where he'll go to stay the night,
>   God in heaven knows.

He rode away from Halland,
　　To Skåne did he wend,
He saw his mother's brother there,
　　He had no better friend.

He saw his mother's brother there,
　　He had no better friend.
And the words were wise that he told to him:
　　That homeward he should wend.

"No, I'll not turn back from here,
　　"Until I've won that maid,
"A court-man true I never knew,
　　"Who feared he'd soon be dead.

"No, I'll never turn back,
　　"Until I've won that wife,
"A court-man true I never knew,
　　"Who feared for his life."

It was Peter Pallebosson,
　　He rode to the rosy grove,
And there he met the king's small boy,
　　Who also there did go.

"Listen up, my fair young man,
　　"To what I ask of you:
"What's the news from the court of the king?
　　"Don't hide it from me now!"

"I have been in the rosy grove,
　　"And led the horses to graze,
"There happens so much in the court of the king,
　　"That to me they never say.

"I have been out under the hills,
  "And led the horses to feed,
"There happens so much in the court of the king,
  "That they never say to me."

From his neck he took a golden chain,
  From his hand a golden ring:
"Now tell me the truth, O little court boy,
  "I'll give you all these things!"

"The horses stand in the stable,
  "All ready for today,
"The king he's gone to the ladies' house,
  "To church they'll be away!

"In Lund's church in Skåne,
  "Are preaching pastors three,
"The king himself will be there today,
  "And there will the maiden be.

"In Lund's church in Skåne,
  "Are preaching pastors ten,
"The king himself will be there today,
  "With all his fierce court men."

It was Peter Pallebosson,
  He let his horse run free,
And all who saw it wondered,
  How the earth held firm beneath.

It was Peter Pallebosson,
  Rode under the hills so green,
And there in the sunlight gleaming bright,
  The golden carriage was seen.

It was Peter Pallebosson,
    In iron he was dressed,
And it was little Kerstin,
    She was so very distressed.

She spoke then, little Kerstin,
    She was so very distressed:
"Tell me who can this rider be,
    "Who comes in iron dressed?"

Answered first her driving-man,
    With reins he held their course:
"It is Sir Peter Pallebosson,
    "I know his dapple-grey horse."

Answered then her serving-maid,
    All-nearest her she sat:
"It is Sir Peter Pallebosson,
    "I know he looks like that!"

And it was Peter Pallebosson,
    To the golden carriage he came,
So fondly he greeted the maiden fair,
    And took her into his arms.

"Ride on now, Peter Pallebosson,
    "You'll only come to harm,
"Behind us rides the king himself,
    "With Sir Nils, my young fast-man."

"I care so little for the king,
    "And Sir Nils, your fast-man, too.
"You'll ride away with me today,
    "If my horse can carry you."

It was Peter Pallebosson,
    With the maiden on his steed,
He rode fifteen Danish miles,
    All at such a speed.

And it was Peter Pallebosson,
    He rode into his yard,
Before him stood his sisters two,
    With curled and plaited hair.

Then spoke his elder sister,
    She was so fair a wife:
"I fear the bride you've brought today,
    "Will cost you your young life."

Then spoke his younger sister,
    She spoke her words so bold:
"I fear the bride you've brought today,
    "Will split both life and soul."

"You're standing here and talking,
    "For much too long a time,
"I'll take my bride away to bed,
    "She's tired from the ride."

Sir Peter and Little Kerstin,
    Away to bed they went,
And after them came the king himself,
    With all his fierce court men.

She sighed then, little Kerstin,
    She was so very afraid:
"Now I can see the king's court men,
    "In iron clad outside."

They beat the door with shields so strong,
    And so with sharpest spears:
"Are you in there, Peter Pallebosson?
    "Then you should come out here!"

They took Sir Peter Pallebosson,
    With his curly yellow hair,
And so they cut his head off,
    Beside the maiden's chair.

And in came young Sir Nils,
    He was then so contented:
"Thank the Lord that I saw the day,
    "I got the one I wanted.

"Listen, little Kerstin,
    "You are a rose so red,
"As a widow I'll take you as readily,
    "As if you were unwed."

"Listen, young Sir Nils,
    "You mustn't think that way!
"As a widow you'll never have me now,
    "Nor if I were still a maid.

"I'll give myself to the cloister,
    "And there my clothes I'll rend,
"There's no man born nor will be born,
    "Who I will have as a friend.

"I'll give myself to the cloister,
    "With all my gold so red,
"And never will that day arrive,
    "I forget Sir Peter's death.

"Underneath my belt I bear,
   "Twin sons fierce and stern,
"And they'll avenge their father's death,
   "The moment that they're born."
You're riding out!

11   SIR SVEDENDAL

The ballad of *Sir Svedendal* is a supernatural romance. It tells the story of a young man, Svedendal, who is cursed to be tormented until he finds a certain girl in a faraway land who he must marry. So he raises his mother from the dead, and she gives him various gifts that will help him in his quest.

Once he has arrived in the foreign land, the young man meets a shepherd, and from him he learns that there is a maiden living there, waiting, also in torment, for a man named Svedendal. The maiden is well guarded, but Svedendal is allowed to enter unhindered, and so both of them are freed from their curse.

This ballad has an unusual significance: the story it tells is the same as that told in an Old Norse poem, and the ballad was instrumental in reuniting the two separated halves of that poem. Nineteenth century ballad scholars realised that the first half of the ballad corresponded to the Old Norse *Grogaldr*, and the second half to the Old Norse *Fjölsvinns-mál*. These two Old Norse poems had been considered separate entities, although they are both about a man named *Svipdag*. Since the link to the ballad was made, they have been treated as the first and second halves of a single poem, known as *Svipdagsmál*.

The translation I present here uses the Swedish version of the ballad as its basis. This Swedish ballad has a great deal in common with Danish versions of the ballad, and several stanzas are identical. There are differences in the particular gifts given to the hero by his dead mother, and also in the detail of how the hero enters the maiden's castle. The Swedish ballad also names the girl as *Spegelklar* (i.e., Mirrorclear). She is unnamed in any of the Danish versions, while in *Svipdagsmål* her name is *Menglöd* (i.e., Necklace glad).

A second Swedish ballad called *Sir Silverdal* tells more or less the same story, but the ballad form is completely different. The *Sir Silverdal* ballad has two-line stanzas rather than the four-line stanzas seen for *Sir Svedendal* and the Danish versions. Thus, the two Swedish ballads represent quite distinct tellings of the story.

It was young Sir Svedendal,
    Was playing with his ball,
He dropped the ball by the maiden's foot,
    It made her cheeks go pale.
You learn and carry your words so well

He dropped the ball by the maiden's foot,
    He followed it on the ground,
But sorrow soon had filled his heart,
    Before the ball he'd found.

"Listen up, young Svedendal:
    "Don't throw your ball to me,
"But throw your ball to a maiden fair,
    "Who longs so much for you!

"And never will you sleep or rest,
    "And peace you'll never find,
"Until you free that maiden fair,
    "Who yearns for you in her mind."

It was young Sir Svedendal,
    He wrapped his head in a skin,
And so he went back into the house,
    To all his court-men in.

"You sit here, all my men,
  "Drink mead from silver bowls,
"While I go up to the high hill,
  "On my mother dear to call.

"You sit here, all my men,
  "Drink mead from silver horns,
"While I go up to the high hill,
  "With my mother dear to talk."

It was young Sir Svedendal,
  To his mother began to call,
So shattered the walls and the marble stones,
  And the hill began to fall.

"Who has come to awaken me?
  "Who's come to call me forth?
"May I never rest in peace,
  "Under the blackest earth?"

"No-one else is waking you,
  "And no-one else will answer,
"Except for me, young Svedendal,
  "Who wants to speak to his mother.

"Listen up, O mother dear,
  "To what I ask of you:
"Where can I find my fast-maid?
  "Don't hide it from me now!"

"This I know for certain,
  "I'll tell it to you now:
"The maiden sits in a foreign land,
  "Waiting there for you.

"I will give you a horse so good,
  "And well he'll carry you forth,
"He runs as well 'cross the salty sea,
  "As over the leaf-green earth.

"And I will give you a sword so good,
  "That by your side will shine,
"And in all the world wherever you go,
  "In comfort you will ride.

"And I will give you gold so red,
  "That in your hands will gleam,
"And when you come to the maiden's hall,
  "She'll know it's you she's seen."

It was young Sir Svedendal,
  He rode in a foreign land,
And there he saw a shepherd good,
  Who drove his sheep on the strand.

"Listen up, good shepherd,
  "To what I ask of you:
"Who owns these sheep you're driving?
  "Don't hide it from me now!"

"Nothing I care for your horse so high,
  "Nor for your gold so red.
"To answer you this is forbidden me,
  "And it would cost my death."

"Listen up, good shepherd,
  "To what I say to you:
"If I become king over all this land,
  "A knight I'll make of you."

"There sits a maiden in her hall,
  "And yearning long she's been,
"All for a man named Svedendal,
  "Who her eyes have never seen.

"All the doors are made of iron,
  "The locks from steel so hard,
"And twelve white bears are lying there,
  "And over the maiden guard."

It was young Sir Svedendal,
  He rode to the maiden's hall,
And all the doors swung open,
  And all the locks did fall.

And all the doors swung open,
  And the locks they fell away,
And the twelve white bears they moved not a hair,
  So very still they lay.

It was young Sir Svedendal,
  Three doors he stepped inside,
And it was maiden Mirrorclear,
  She met him with her eyes.

And it was maiden Mirrorclear,
  She took him into her arms:
"And for our winnings we shall have,
  "This land and all this realm!"
You learn and carry your words so well

12 | KING SPELEMAN

The details of the early days of the Scandinavian Medieval Ballad tradition are lost. It seems that the tradition and many songs were already established well before the first full ballad texts were written down (in Danish) in the 1500s. But only clues and fragments are left to suggest information about that time. And some of these appear in rather unexpected places.

When the Danish mapmaker Claudius Clavus was drawing his map of Greenland in the early 1400s, he did not mark place-names on the map. Instead, he marked the features along the coastline with the text of the first stanza of a ballad, with the words of the lyric alternating between headlands and inlets. Claudius Clavus's original map does not survive, but a copy made by Nicolaus Germanus in the 1460s does.

This so-called Greenland stanza corresponds very closely to the first stanza of a ballad written down later in a rather fuller form in Swedish. The Swedish ballad is called *King Speleman*, and is translated here.

The ballad itself is a short tale of loyal service by a boy, Otter, to his master, King Speleman. When Speleman gets into trouble in a fight, he calls on Otter for help. Otter comes to his aid very effectively, and is well rewarded for his service.

There lived a fighter in Helsingborg,
 King Speleman he was called,
He surely owned more chests of silver,
 Than others had fatty pork.
The rainy wind drives north
 And the sea from the south goes north

There lived another by Davidskär,
 He was, though, much less wealthy,
Eleven were the sons he had,
 And all were fighters worthy.

It was fighter Tyresson,
 He carried his sword in his hand:
"Say, will you give me your daughter dear,
 "Or will you flee the land?"

King Speleman answered with words so sharp,
 Like he was cross with him:
"I won't give you my daughter dear,
 "For you are a fighter grim."

"Either you'll take to the water with me,
 "Reddest gold to find,
"Or you'll come to the hills with me,
 "With eleven brothers to fight."

"No I'll not take to the water with you,
 "Reddest gold to find,
"But rather I'll go to the hills with you,
 "With eleven brothers to fight."

The first attack together they took,
 In front of Tyre the fighter,
King Speleman's forehead soon was hit,
 And at that, he grew whiter.

King Speleman called to Otter his boy:
"Help me in my distress!
"And you'll not wear grey woollen clothes,
"While we have silk of the best!"

Boy Otter out through the door he sprang,
With a stick he barred the door,
And he tore an oak up by the roots,
The foremost and first he saw.

And Otter took the oak in his hands,
He lifted it up on his back,
Eleven fighters he struck down,
In his foremost and first attack.

Eleven fighters he struck down,
And sent them to their death,
And then he went to King Speleman's court,
And cut the silk so red.

Eleven fighters he struck down,
And laid them at his feet,
And then he went to King Speleman's court,
And cut the silk so white.

Eleven fighters he struck down,
And all the same they died,
And then he went to King Speleman's court,
And called himself Otter the wise.
The rainy wind drives north
And the sea from the south goes north

KING SPELEMAN

13 | HOLGER DANE AND BURMAN

At Floda church in Sweden, the ceilings are covered in frescoes.

The church in Floda has a remarkable story. The old church was rebuilt in the 1400s, and a vaulted ceiling was added. This was decorated with frescoes by the artist Albertus Pictor around 1480. The church building has been rebuilt, damaged, and rebuilt again since then. And from the outside, it now appears to be a neogothic brick-built structure that was put up in the 1880s. But despite this, the medieval interior remains intact. And the late-medieval vaulted-ceiling frescoes remain in very good condition more than 500 years on.

Unsurprisingly, the great majority of the paintings show biblical scenes. But the paintings are also interesting for ballad enthusiasts. A group of four paintings in the fourth bay of the vaulted ceiling shows (with labels by the artist) David killing Goliath; Widrick Waylandsson (Wideke Welandsson) fighting Diderick of Bern; Sven Felding (Sven Fötlink) killing a troll; and Holger Dane killing Burman. It seems that at least some of these four paintings, and possibly all of them, illustrate scenes from medieval ballads; the paintings are older than any surviving written full ballad texts. The most convincing evidence that ballads are actually being portrayed comes the fact that the chorus (*omkväde*) line *Holger Dane he won victory over Burman* is painted underneath the picture of the hero.

The ballads of *Holger Dane and Burman*, and of *Sven Felding* are in-

81

cluded in this collection. Widrick Waylandsson and Diderick of Bern appear in *Warrior Lore*, but there, far from fighting each other, they are allies. A Swedish ballad of *David and Goliath* is also known.

Immediately alongside the paintings of ballad heroes, another painting in the vaulted church roof at Floda shows a scene with St Olaf standing in a ship, speaking to a group of trolls. This painting too could be an illustration of a ballad scene, this time from the ballad *St Olaf's Sailing Race*. In the ballad, the ship is called *Oxen*, and the ship in the painting is drawn with an ox's head for its figurehead. In the ballad an archer shoots an arrow to pull the ship back into the sea, and also in the painting there is an archer standing in the stern of the ship. It is tempting to speculate that Albertus Pictor had the ballad of St Olaf in mind when he painted this scene. It certainly seems to illustrate something of the same story that is told in the ballad. A translation of *St Olaf's Sailing Race* is also included in this book.

Holger Dane sits asleep in a vault under Kronborg Castle at Helsingör with his beard grown fast to the ground. But the story goes that the day Denmark is in peril, he will emerge to save his country. Thus Holger Dane has a role like that of King Arthur in Britain — as a so-called king under the mountain.

Holger Dane became widely known in Scandinavia around the end of the medieval era, and part of his fame was surely due to his role as a ballad hero. This ballad describes his fight against a fearful opponent, the giant Burman.

Burman arrives on the scene demanding the hand of the daughter of the King of Issland in marriage. But as the chorus (*omkväde*) of the song tells us, things do not go well for Burman in the end. Luckily for the King, champion fighter Holger Dane is close at hand, and he can call on him for help: Holger has been held in one of his prisons for the past fifteen years. And luckily, when the King's daughter Gloria goes to the prison to fetch Holger, our hero is all too willing to help the cause by fighting Burman.

Holger Dane is an unusual Scandinavian hero in that the stories about him seem to have been told first in the southern European legends of

Charlemagne, and then made their way north through translations from French in *Karlamagnus Saga* (*Charlemagne's Saga*), and *Olger Danskes Krönike* (*Holger Dane's Chronicle*). Holger appears in the French *Song of Roland*, and he is the main character of the French chanson de geste *Chevalerie d'Ogier de Danemarche*. So famous was he in medieval France that he is commonly identified as one of the named characters that appear on French playing cards — the Jack of Spades in the French national deck. There is a record that gives an idea of who the historical Holger Dane was: In an old chronicle from St Martin's abbey in Cologne, it is written that in 778, after being destroyed by the Saxons, the abbey was rebuilt by *Olgerus dux Daniae*, i.e., Holger, leader of the Danes, with the help of Charlemagne.

Burman stood outside the town,
   He let his weapons shine:
"Now listen up, O Issland's King,
   "Your daughter will be mine!"
Holger Dane won victory over Burman

The King he walked outside the town,
   He lifted up his hat:
"Where do you come from, mighty man?
   "None of us here know that."

"I am come from Spåre Land,
   "And there I have my friends,
"And you will know me in this town,
   "Before my time here ends."

Burman rode outside the town,
   He looked out to the west:
"Come out and see, Miss Gloria,
   "How well I ride a horse."

83

"You're not so very fine to see,
   "Your shirt is plain and white,
"Your crooked nose is two feet long,
   "A gargoyle you are like."

Burman pulled his horse around,
   His lance it shone so bright,
He cast a stone towards the town,
   As big as a bathing hut.

The maiden she went to her father,
   She spoke to her father so:
"Now trouble's come to both of us,
   "You'll tell me what to do!"

"If we should search around the world,
   "No fighter's help we'd find,
"Except from only Holger Dane,
   "Who wins in every fight."

The maiden she cried so loud a cry,
   Over the prison hall:
"Are you in here, Holger Dane,
   "And can you walk at all?"

"Very little can I walk,
   "Hardly can I crawl,
"Here I have lain for fifteen years,
   "In your father's prison hall.

"Here I have lain for fifteen years,
   "In iron bound and chained,
"But tell me now, Miss Gloria,
   "What's worrying your mind?"

"Burman has come here to us,
  "A mighty fighter's name,
"He'll drive my father from the land,
  "And carry me off in shame!"

"Burman's not the man for you,
  "He'll not take you away.
"His mother is a sea-troll,
  "Far in the east she stays.

"I'll tell you now of Burman,
  "Of Burman's size of course,
"Fifteen feet he stands in height,
  "Higher than saddle and horse.

"I'll tell you more of Burman,
  "Of Burman's sword so long,
"Fifteen feet it is in length,
  "Between the tip and the tang.

"If I could have a horse to ride,
  "And sword and armour too,
"Then I would ride a joust today,
  "To risk my life for you."

"Well I will give you clothes so new,
  "All the best, of course,
"And I will give you weapons too,
  "And also saddle and horse."

Burman rode outside the town,
  His tail was hanging low:
"I'm afraid it's Holger Dane,
  "The fiercest man I know."

And so they rode the first ride,
    As foes they rode around,
Their lances soon were shattered,
    And their horses fell to the ground.

Holger drew his blazing blade,
    It gleamed like gold so red,
And he cut Burman's head in two,
    And soon to death he'd bled.

Holger rode outside the town,
    He let his weapons shine.
"Now listen up, O Issland's King,
    "Your daughter will be mine!"

"I have no daughters more than one,
    "She doesn't have a man,
"You set her free from Burman,
    "And you shall have her hand."

"Today I've played with Burman,
    "He didn't last too long,
"Yes we have played and fought today,
    "Like two boys fierce and strong."

"Is this the truth you say to me?
    "And not a lie you tell?
"I'll let you have my daughter then,
    "And half my lands as well."
Holger Dane won victory over Burman

HOLGER DANE AND BURMAN

14 | SVEN FELDING

Sven Felding is a legendary hero in Denmark. He is especially well known for his great size, and for having the strength of twelve men. There are gigantic cauldrons, swords, and drinking horns in Denmark that are supposed to have belonged to him.

There are at least two stories about how Sven Felding got his great strength. One tells of how a troll granted Sven Felding the strength of twelve men if he would help him fight a second troll who took the form of an ox. Sven Felding helped the troll, and defeated the ox, so he was allowed to keep his new strength.

In the second, Sven Felding met a group of dancing elves. One of them asked him to drink from a horn she gave to him. But Sven Felding was suspicious, and he threw the contents of the horn at a horse, which was singed by the liquid. Sven Felding then rode off with the horn, with the elf in hot pursuit, anxious to get back the horn. She promised to grant Sven Felding the strength of twelve men if he gave her back the horn. And on that condition he did return the horn to her.

This ballad tells a different story about Sven Felding, and how he was able to defeat a troll while he was away on a pilgrimage. This troll is particularly distinguished by its diet — it preferred to eat only ladies and maidens.

It isn't clear whether the more decisive element of Sven Felding's plan to beat the troll is the attachment of a holy object to his lance, or the brute-force approach of using a very big lance indeed. Perhaps there is room to draw one's own conclusions. But certainly it seems that with this two-fold assault the troll didn't stand much of a chance.

There is a story of how one time in Norway, three ministers were up for a vacancy at a parish church. As part of the selection process, they were asked to sing for the assembled congregation. Two of them sang hymns or psalms, but the third struck up with the well known ballad of Sven Felding. The congregation loved it, and he got the job.

Sven Felding he sits in Helsingör,
    Boasting of deeds so grand,
And there he sits, both gentle and mild,
    His sword held in his hand.

He said he'd make a pilgrimage,
    To Rome his way he'd wend:
"And every man who follows me,
    "Lodging he will find."

The first night that he stayed away,
    He stayed in Hertigensö,
He stayed at the house of a maiden fair,
    They held each other so dear.

At the highest table she let him sit,
    Above the knights and the men,
And then she asked, this maiden fair,
    From whereabouts he'd come.

She saw then that Sven Felding's shirt,
    Was sewn with gold the best:
"This is not a pilgrim poor,
    "We have here as our guest."

"No, this is not a pilgrim poor,
  "We have here as our guest,
"But it's the King of Denmark,
  "Or another one of the best."

"I'm not the King of Denmark,
  "I'm not so very grand,
"I am a lowly farmer's son,
  "Born here in the land.

"Listen up, my maiden fair:
  "You mustn't be misled,
"There are so many children born,
  "And each one has his strength."

And so it was the maiden fair,
  She sewed the silken seams,
But with every stitch that that the maiden sewed,
  Her eyes were running in streams.

"Listen now, my maiden fair,
  "What are you sorrowing over?
"Say, have you found your father dead?
  "Or have you lost your lover?"

"I haven't found my father dead,
  "I haven't lost my lover,
"There is a troll here in this town,
  "And the town he's turning over."

"There is a troll here in our town,
  "He's laying the town to waste,
"And nothing else will he have for food,
  "But ladies and maidens to taste!

"There is a troll here in our town,
    "And the town will be destroyed,
"Unless there is a Christian man,
    "Who dares a joust to ride."

"Well here you'll have a Christian man,
    "Who dares a joust to ride,
"If only I could find a horse,
    "On which I can rely."

The maiden she led out fifteen foals,
    And all of them white as snow.
Sven Felding he laid his saddle on them,
    And they sank to the earth below.

And so there came a miller man,
    He spoke as well as he could:
"I say I have a little brown foal,
    "He stands in the willow-tree woods.

"Yes I have a little brown foal,
    "He stands in the willow-tree woods,
"And if I could trade him for one of these,
    "Then let him run I would!"

And when the little brown foal came forth,
    He was just as the miller had said:
His teeth were white, his body was broad,
    And high he held his head.

Sven Felding he pulled off his gloves so small,
    His hands they were snow white,
He tightened his saddle girth himself,
    On the swains he shouldn't rely.

He tightened the saddle girth overly tight,
    The way it suited him well,
The horse before him fell to its knees,
    And the saddle girth snapped as well.

"I have fifteen good gold rings,
    "Here with me I've taken.
"If I could get a saddle girth,
    "I'd let these rings be broken."

Fifteen were the maidens fair,
    With silk they wove and sewed,
So they could make a saddle girth,
    To bear Sven Felding's load.

'Twas early in the morning,
    When the saddle girth was made,
Well six feet long and a quarter thick,
    And also two feet wide.

Sven Felding he pulled off his gloves so small,
    His hands they were snow white,
He tightened his saddle girth himself,
    On the swains he shouldn't rely.

He tightened the saddle girth overly tight,
    It suited him well and good.
The horse before him fell to its knees,
    Sven Felding he understood.

"Now I see, my good horse,
    "That like a man you're wise,
"So I will loosen you a touch,
    "Before I mount to ride."

And so he loosened him a touch,
    The horse became so glad.
And so it was Sven Felding,
    He sat upon his back.

The first ride together they rode,
    The fighters both were strong,
Sven Felding's lance it broke in two,
    His shield to the ground was flung.

Sven Felding then he made a plan,
    The way he'd win was clear:
"Meet me tomorrow again on the field,
    "I surely will be here."

"I'll lay aside this little lance,
    "That men in the land can move,
"Instead I'll carry a ship's mast,
    "And this I intend to use!"

And so Sven Felding he went to church,
    And there he did confess.
And there upon his lance's shaft
    He set the holy bread.

The second ride together they rode,
    The fighters rode in wrath,
The troll's neck it broke in two,
    And down he fell on the heath.

The troll's neck it broke in two,
    His back in pieces three.
Sven Felding he rode to the maiden fair,
    To toast the victory.

Out then rode the maiden's knights,
    And lifted him from his horse:
"Land and riches we'll give to you,
    "And the maiden to marry of course."

"My fast-maid lives in Denmark,
    "So much she cares for me.
"For seven barrels of reddest gold,
    "That maid I'd not betray.

"But say that you now will build a house,
    "Below by Hertigensö,
"And say that if any pilgrim comes,
    "He will find lodging there.

"If any Danish pilgrims come,
    "Spare neither wine nor bread,
"And pray well for Sven Felding's soul,
    "When he has long been dead."

15 | ST OLAF'S SAILING RACE

King Olaf II Haraldsson is known as the patron saint and eternal King of Norway, credited with converting the country to Christianity. King Harald Hardrada is known as the last viking king. And the two of them were half-brothers. A contest between these two figures seems to have been a tempting prospect for ballad composers.

The ballad *St Olaf's Sailing Race* describes a bet between the two brothers: they agree to have a sailing race, with the winner becoming King of Norway. Despite Harald's advantages — he insists on swapping ships so that he has the faster one, and also has a big head start — St Olaf has God on his side. So he is able to take his ship on a short-cut across the land (or through the air). The trolls he meets are turned to stone, and St Olaf arrives first to the finishing post in Trondheim.

The sailing race described here as a bet for the Norwegian throne is certainly a fiction. Although the two men were half-brothers by the same mother, Olaf was around twenty years older than Harald. Olaf was king rather earlier than Harald (with several more Kings of Norway in between the two), so the idea that Olaf should emerge victorious from such a contest does not make much sense. Rather it seems to be the ideas that St Olaf represents and embodies that must compete with the ideas represented by Harald Hardarada in this race for Norway's future.

Although this ballad is very Norwegian in its setting and its relevance, it is translated here from Danish versions, which survive in much less fragmentary form than Norwegian (or Swedish) versions. In fact, St Olaf was a popular cult figure throughout medieval Scandinavia, and pilgrims would go to Trondheim to visit his grave.

The names of the two ships, *Oxen* and *Ormen*, mean *The Ox* and *The Dragon*.

> St Olaf the King and Harald his brother,
>> For Norway's crown they raced each other.
> *It's so beautiful resting in Trondheim*
>
> "The first of us to reach the end,
>> "He will be king over Norway's land.
>
> "Whichever of us the best can sail,
>> "He will be king over fell and dale."
>
> "If I'm to sail with you today,
>> "Then we must swap our ships, I say.
>
> "Ormen she sails as fast as the sky,
>> "Oxen she sails so slowly by.
>
> "If you sail with Ormen the fast,
>> "How can I with Oxen race?"
>
> "If you think my ship is better than yours,
>> "Then yes you may take mine of course.
>
> "Ormen the fast you can take,
>> "With Oxen the slow I will race.
>
> "But first to the churchyard we shall go,
>> "Before we move our sails and oars.
>
> "First I must hear masses three,
>> "Before I sail upon the sea."
>
> And into the church St Olaf was gone,
>> His hair like noble gold it shone.

And soon the word to St Olaf came:
"Your brother, Harald, has sailed away."

"Let him sail if sail he will,
"To God's word will we listen still.

"Let him sail if sail he may,
"The word of God we will obey.

"The mass it is the word of the Lord,
"Bring water to the benches broad.

"We'll sit at the benches and we'll eat,
"And then down on the strand we'll meet."

St Olaf he walked upon the strand,
Where Oxen lay upon the sand.

And then down to the strand they bore,
Their sails, their anchors, and their oars.

St Olaf he stood in Oxen's prow,
"In Jesus' name, sail onward now!"

St Olaf he took hold of Oxen's horn,
"Sail on as though you sailed for home!"

And Oxen began to sail so fast,
And the wake rose high as they sailed past.

A small boy was sent to climb the mast:
"See if Harald can be passed."

"No more of Ormen can I see,
"Than a little twig of an oaken tree."

St Olaf he beat on Oxen's side:
"Much faster through the sea you'll drive!"

St Olaf he struck at Oxen's eye:
"Much faster you'll go sailing by!"

Then Oxen began to rock and sway,
So the men on the benches couldn't stay.

St Olaf he took a rope and a line,
And so he tied his boatsmen down.

Then the steersman shouted out:
"And where will we be sailing now?"

St Olaf he pulled off his gloves so small,
And he himself went to the wheel.

"Over the hills and the cliffs we'll sail,
"Wherever we find the shortest way!"

And so they sailed over hills and fells,
And out ran all the little trolls.

The old woman stood with her spindle and wheel:
"Why have you sailed to upset us here?

"St Olaf with your yellow beard,
"Through my cellar wall you've steered!"

St Olaf in reply did say:
"Stand and be a boulder grey."

"Stand there, troll, and turn to stone,
"Until I come this way again!"

He set his bow against his knee,
The arrow hit the tall sails-tree.

He shot an arrow from the prow,
And Oxen back to the sea did go.

101

So great was St Olaf's faith in the Lord,
That he arrived three days before.

St Olaf he was a God-fearing man,
So he became king of Norway's land.
It's so beautiful resting in Trondheim

Notes

It is most often the case that several versions of each ballad are known. The degree of variation is sometimes small, sometimes large. Sometimes the difference may lie in whether someone was wearing a white shirt or a silken shirt. Sometimes it may be a name that has changed. Sometimes there may be major differences in the plot of the story.

And there are further complications. Almost inevitably, stanzas will be forgotten by singers. Sometimes, a long ballad can have parts that do not quite follow, and some ballads were only written down in fragmentary form. Comparison of different versions of a ballad can make it clear how the pieces fit together. Thus in preparing each of these ballad translations, I have not used only one source. Several versions have been consulted. This gives a certain degree of flexibility that allows the preparation of translations that work well in English.

In addition to the stories told in the ballads, rhyme, metre, and repeated motifs contribute to the ballad texts. But although rhyme is a major defining feature of the ballad verse, the rhymes in the Scandinavian ballads are not always perfect: often they are half-rhymes, and occasionally there is no rhyme at all. Similarly, the metre is not always uniform, though a sung rhythm may be. The fact that these "rules" are not hard and fast makes translating the ballads a lot easier than it might be otherwise.

Repetition is quite an important feature of these ballads. Repetition is probably an important feature that helps singers to memorise the ballads. But it is also important for an audience, as it helps them to anticipate and feel familiar with what is happening. The repetition can take different forms. Most simply, there are short phrases, sometimes alliterative, that are used often and repeatedly: things like "palfrey grey" for a horse, or "billowy blue" for the sea.

Whole stanzas are often repeated with minor alterations within a single ballad. For example, from *Peter Pallebosson*:

> In Lund's church in Skåne,
>> Are preaching pastors three,
> The king himself will be there today,
>> And there will the maiden be.

> In Lund's church in Skåne,
>> Are preaching pastors ten,
> The king himself will be there today,
>> With all his fierce court men.

And sometimes very similar stanzas appear in different ballads. For example, from *Heming and King Harald* (*Warrior Lore*):

> So they hoisted high the silken sails,
>> Upon the gilded masts,
> And didn't let those sails be struck,
>> Till Aslack's land they passed.

And from *Asmund Frægdegjevar*:

> They hoisted high the silken sail,
>> Up to the the gilded spar,
> And it wasn't struck to the benches down,
>> Till Trollbotten they saw.

The ballads were sung with repeated chorus lines called the *omkväde*. These are given in italics for the first and last stanzas of each of the ballads. The omkväde could be a line or lines that were sung after each stanza (common for four-line stanzas), or alternatively the omkväde lines could be interspersed with the other lines of the stanza (especially for two-line stanzas). The omkväde lines are closely associated with the music of the ballad.

The ballads are written in verse, but the language is almost always straightforward. The ballads achieve their powerful point without using florid, poetic language. So in translation, a similarly simple English language must be preferable. I have also avoided the use of archaic words.

Having said that, a couple of possibly obscure terms must be mentioned. I have used "fast-man" and "fast-maid" to represent the Swedish *fästeman* and *fästemö* (or their equivalent terms in Danish and Norwegian). These terms are used to refer to a man and woman in a state of formal engagement to be married, or in an alternative to church marriage.

A common way of referring to a horse is as a *gångare*, and this I have given as "palfrey". It almost always occurs as the alliterative *gångare grå* (i.e., "palfrey grey"). The word literally means "walker", as opposed to a "runner" or "charger" in the less common *rennare röd*.

It sometimes happens that units of measurement are used in the ballads, especially to describe the grotesque enormity of trolls or sometimes the great and glorious size of heroes. The *aln* is one such old Swedish unit. I have sometimes given these measurements in feet, and occasionally used the equivalent old English unit of an *ell*.

The spellings of names in the ballad sources are quite irregular. Most often I have used a spelling that is representative of the name as it appears. Occasionally I have translated into English: thus, *Holger Dansk* is *Holger Dane*; *Solfager* is *Sunfair*; *Spegelklar* is *Mirrorclear*; I have used *The Dragon King* for *Ormekonungen*, but *Orm the Strong* for *Ormen Stark*. *Sigurd* and his horse *Grane* appear in the Norwegian ballad with their Norwegian spellings, which may be more familiar. But in Danish, I have used *Sivard* and *Greyman*. The hero's name is pretty consistent as *Sivar* or *Sivard* across Danish as well as Swedish ballads. The name of the horse is rather more variable, but certainly the first element means "grey".

The way that ballads were recorded and preserved varied between the different Scandinavian countries as a result of local fashions, politics, and the enthusiasm of individuals. Danish ballads were first written down in courtly songbooks from around 1550. Norwegian ballads were almost not written down at all until collectors in the 1800s travelled around the country to find places where the oral tradition was still alive. In Sweden, ballads appear in courtly songbooks dating from shortly after the first Danish manuscripts, and contemporary notations were published in the 1800s. Ballads were passed on orally, but, broadside editions of some ballads were known, and Vedel published a popular ballad compilation (known as *Kämpevisabogen* or *Hundredvisebogen*) in 1591.

I have used ballad sources as reprinted in the following publications: A. I. Arwidsson, *Svenska Fornsånger* (1834–1842); E. G. Geijer and A. A. Afzelius, *Svenska Folkvisor Från Forntiden* (1814–1816); The online Ballad Archive of the Norwegian Dokumentasjonsprosjektet; M. B. Landstad, *Norske Folkeviser* (1853); and S. Grundtvig, *Danmarks Gamle Folkeviser* (1853).

Åsmund Frægdegjeva — From Norwegian *Åsmund Fregdegjeva*, from the Ballad Archive and from Landstad No. 1.

Steinfinn Fefinnson — From Norwegian *Steinfinn Fefinnson*, from the Ballad Archive and from Landstad No. 4.

Esbjörn Proud and Orm the Strong — From Swedish *Essbjörn Prude och Ormen Stark*, from Arwidsson No. 8 (A: *manuscript MS, Stockholm*, and B: *manuscript WB, Stockholm*). My translation is based on A; version B is very similar. The Faeroese ballad *Brusajøkils Kvad* mentioned in the text tells a similar story, but there is little or no lyrical overlap.

Sunfair and the Dragon King — From Norwegian *Solfager og Ormekongen*, from the Ballad Archive and from Landstad No. 56, with stanzas from Swedish *Jungfru Solfager*, from Arwidsson No. 25 (A: *manuscript MS, Stockholm*, and B: collected in Värmland och Dal).

Bendik and Årolilja — From Norwegian *Bendik og Årolilja*, from the Ballad Archive.

Sigurd Sven — From Norwegian *Sigurd Svein*, from the Ballad Archive and from Landstad No. 9.

Sivard Snare Sven — From Danish *Sivard Snarensvend*, from Grundtvig No. 2 (A: *Langebeks Foliohandskrift*, and B: *Sophia Sandbergs Handskrift*).

My translation ends as for Grundtvig A; the ending of version B is similar. But there is another variant of this Danish ballad (see Grundtvig C) in which Sivard does not survive the leap over the wall.

A corresponding Swedish ballad is known, though it seems not to be well preserved: *Herr Sibohl* (also in Grundtvig). Again, the hero is given a horse, *Gramen*, by his mother and rides away to a castle. But from then on, the story is different: he serves at the king's court and marries his daughter.

Little Lisa — My translation closely follows *Herr Redevall*, from Geijer & Afzelius No. 58, with some stanzas from *Krist Lilla och Herr Tidemann*, from Arwidsson No. 54A (collected in Värmland), and *Lilla Lisa*, from *Södermanlands Äldre Kulturhistoria*, vol. 5, No. 30.

Sven Norman and Miss Gullborg — From Norwegian *Svein Nordmann* and *Rullemann og Hilleborg*, both from the Ballad Archive.

Peter Pallebosson — From Swedish *Peder Pallebogson*, from Arwidsson No. 30 (A: *manuscript WB, Stockholm*, and B: *Verelianska Samlingen*).

Sir Svedendal — From Swedish *Unge Herr Svedendal*, from Arwidsson No. 143 (*Varelianska Handskriften*), with some lines from Danish *Ungen Svejdal*, from Grundtvig No. 70 (B–D).

King Speleman — From Swedish *Kung Speleman*, from Arwidsson No. 10 (*Varelianska Samlingen*).

Holger Dane and Burman — From Swedish *Olger Dansk och Burman*, from Arwidsson No. 7 (A: *Gyllenmars Visbok*, and B: broadsides). My translation mainly follows A with some lines from B. Note that the Danish ballad *Holger Danske og Burmand*, Grundtvig No. 30, is not too similar to the two Swedish versions of the ballad.

Sven Felding — From Danish *Svend Felding*, from Grundtvig No. 31 (A: *Karen Brahes Foliohandskrift*, B: *Magdalena Barnewitz Handskrift*, and C: *Vedel*), and Swedish *Sven Färling*, from Arwidsson No. 14 (collected in Värmland och Dal), and *Sven Fotling* (*Verelianska Samlingen*).

For my translation of *Sven Felding*, I used rather more "reconstruction" than for any of the other ballads in this collection. The two surviving Swedish versions of the ballad are just fragments (in one, there is an explanation of some forgotten stanzas in the middle of the transcript, and it is written also that the ending is missing), but both correspond to parts of better-preserved Danish versions of the ballad. So the first part of the ballad translation, leading up to the first fight between Sven Felding and the troll, uses the two Swedish fragments as well as Danish versions. The end of the ballad comes entirely from Danish versions.

St Olaf's Sailing Race — From Danish *Hellig-Olavs Væddefart*, from Grundtvig No. 50 (A: *Vedel*, and B: *Svanings Handskrift*), with some lines from Swedish *St Olofs Kappsegling*, from E. Wigström (Gothenburg, 1881), and Norwegian from the Ballad Archive.